THIS MUSIC

for
Professor Kantrowitz,

JD

ABOUT THE AUTHOR

Lewis Dimmick received his MFA in Creative Writing from New York University, where he was nominated by Galway Kinnell for Poetry Magazine's Ruth Lilly Fellowship. He teaches writing for The City University of New York.

THIS MUSIC
Pieces on Heavy Metal, Punk Rock, and Hardcore Punk

Lewis Dimmick

Wardance
NYC, 2013

Copyright © 2013 by Lewis Dimmick

WAR 15

ALL RIGHTS RESERVED

For information about permission to reproduce selections from this book, write to

Freddy Alva, P.O. Box 770451, Woodside, NY 11377

ISBN 978-0-615-78288-1

Printed in the United States of America

10 9 8 7 6 5 4 3 2 1

www.wardancerecords.com

Title Page Art by Elias Martinez

Cover Layout by Liz Hill

for my mother

CONTENTS

I

Otherworldly — 3

II

The Doty Avenue Dirtbags — 9
Sweet Leaf — 10
Dazed And Confused — 11
Satan, Father — 12
My Hair — 13
What Is This — 17
Slave To The Power — 18

III

Sightseeing — 23
Finally — 24
Outerwear — 25
Sunday Is Gloomy — 26
Sign Of The Times — 27
17 April 1988, CBGB's — 28
I Got A Right — 30
In One City — 32
An Understanding — 34

IV

At The Movies — 37
Victim In Pain — 39
Dave Insurgent — 42

V

Out There — 49
Full Force — 50
Demo Demo — 51
Our Gang Live On WNYU — 53
Looking Out — 55
Going Off — 56
Sitting Around The Fire — 57
17 July 2010 — 58

VI

A Brief, Quiet Moment — 63
Where I Was — 64
The Soul Is The Force — 65
This Music — 66

I

OTHERWORLDLY

> I have now won from the world
> my world. The former immensity
> of others, becomes today
> my immensity.
> —Juan Ramon Jimenez

Growing up, Hobi was my best friend. We lived in the same building, I on the second floor and he on the sixth. His apartment was unique. His father collected records; he owned thousands, most of them picture discs and colored vinyl; they were everywhere. There were huge subway posters on the walls and amazing stereo equipment in the living room, where his dad lived and slept. It was a fascinating place.

Frank was a character. Whenever I'd call, he'd answer the phone, "House of flies, we don't serve trade-ins." He was a great artist; Hobi showed me old drawings and paintings he still had stashed around the apartment. I loved hanging out up there. We took the living room over when Frank was gone, listening to records on his high-end audio gear. It made an impression on me, the feeling I got that the audio equipment was the most important thing in the house. Music was essential.

My earliest exposure to punk rock and hardcore was in that apartment. One of the records Hobi and I seized on early was *The Great Rock 'n' Roll Swindle* by The Sex Pistols. I was intrigued by the back cover, which featured the words "Who Killed Bambi" scrawled in blood red over a photo of a dead deer with an arrow in its neck. That cover was like a window into another world, where the curtain of pretense had been lifted and the harsh and the real had come into view; it declared itself as apart from the mainstream. The song itself, "Who Killed Bambi," was goofy and cartoonish, something that would appeal to children, but with the snarl of a punk attitude in it, which also declared itself as apart.

These were new discoveries. It was 1982. I was twelve years old.

There was a lot to look at inside the gatefold: live band shots, naked punk girls, cartoons of Sid Vicious wearing a red shirt with a black swastika on it. I knew intuitively the shirt was for shock value; I knew the record had nothing to do with racism. In that respect I suppose I "got" punk immediately. This was different from my previous experience with music, which involved AC/DC, Black Sabbath, Iron Maiden. "Friggin' In The Riggin'" was vulgar and bizarre. "My Way" was a snotty epic.

We also found among Frank's collection a Sid Vicious solo record, the cover of which featured a photo of Sid wearing a chain with a lock around his neck. Hobi adopted this look all throughout junior high school. "Must you wear that stuff to school *every* day?" our science teacher, Mrs. Luigi, begged. In addition to the chain with the lock, he would wear a pin on his shirt that read, "Sex, Drugs, & Rock 'n' Roll."

In God We Trust, Inc. by The Dead Kennedys was another crucial discovery. The band name being in such bad taste left no room for doubt: this was punk; but shock value was not the beginning and the end here.

The front cover featured an image of Jesus on a cross. The cross was made of dollar bills and topped with a bar code. The back cover showed two elderly women pointing and smiling at a Klan rally outside the window of their car. I liked that, even before I heard the music, the record was suggesting strong, controversial ideas. It was bold and courageous. It had guts.

The first song, "Religious Vomit," was stunning. The hard crunch of the guitars and crash of the drums set loose a burst of speed and jumbled lyrics that went racing toward its end right from the start and didn't let up one bit till it got there. This was hardcore: efficiency of form, nothing wasted. It was intense. Jello Biafra sounded like an infuriated circus clown. "All religions make me wanna throw up / All religions make me sick / All religions make me wanna throw up / All religions suck." When another friend from school brought this record into his house, his mother crushed it and threw it in the garbage. Its ability to offend wasn't what I loved about it though. I loved that anything could exist inside a song, any viewpoint, any tone. I loved the directness. What shocked me most was that after one minute and eleven seconds, the song, which had been moving at top speed the entire time, came to the most sudden of stops. It was so short, yet there were so many words, with so much meaning. The quiet when it ended seemed amplified. It was truly stunning.

Yet another record that changed the world of my youth was the compilation *Rat Music For Rat People*, the first volume. Through that record I discovered Bad Brains.

H.R. seemed to become a different person every few seconds in a song like "How Low Can A Punk Get?" and each one of those people was capable of incredible things. He was explosive and dynamic, hooting and howling and grunting and jabbering. It was unlike anything else in existence.

The music we heard in Frank's collection inspired Hobi and me to buy guitars, to learn, by degrees, to tune them, to play them, to write songs. I remember one night in particular, early in our apprenticeship, we wrote two songs in one sitting. When we were done we went to the store to buy snacks. It was snowing outside. Early in the morning, dark and quiet. It was a new world. I think we felt more part of it. We had offered something up to it. We knew there were others out there like us, people that did what we did. We felt their presence through the dark. We were now members of their tribe.

II

THE DOTY AVENUE DIRTBAGS

I was walking home when I heard the sound, alive behind a garage door.

I couldn't move.

This was on Doty Avenue in South Beach, Staten Island, home to "The Doty Avenue Dirtbags," filthy-faced kids who cursed you and threw rocks at you as you walked home from the arcade.

I had never heard live music before, not in person: the volume; the richness.

It was like I had previously only seen images of the sky, and here now was the sky itself.

I couldn't move.

SWEET LEAF

South Beach, Staten Island—in the late '70s, early '80s—was a metal neighborhood. Imagine a bunch of longhairs in denim and leather standing around drinking beer.

A silver boombox with black speakers sat at someone's boots. Someone coughed.

The cough started out rough; it sounded like the person was gagging. I looked around to see who it was, but when I did the cough froze in time and began to echo, increasing in volume as if soaring through space.

Then music broke in, fuzzy and warm, deep and soulful.

It was not as I had thought. No one on the street was coughing. I mistook the music for life itself.

Brief moments of utter confusion seem to spread out over great lengths of time. Now I returned to earth; I returned to things I could understand.

This was the music of the gods; the tone of the gods; the groove of the gods.

DAZED AND CONFUSED

My sister, right after she graduated high school, imposed upon herself a sudden transformation.

Bare-chested Robert Plant came down from her wall and in his place went framed prints of colorful flowers.

Not too colorful though. They blended in.

Her transition was seamless; this was "growing up."

I wasn't convinced, but watched her go full steam into her new life.

The records I once marveled at in her room, Led Zeppelin, Black Sabbath, AC/DC—these were mine now.

I carried them off like bars of gold.

SATAN, FATHER

I once owned a Venom picture disc. It was shaped like the devil's head: horns, pointy beard. It was a cool-looking devil, too; he wore a dark smirk. The image was so striking that I asked my friend Hobi to paint it on the back of my denim jacket.

I remember my mother walked past us, surveying his work.

"That's nice," she said.

Later, when she and I were alone, she asked me calmly if I worshipped the devil.

I answered that I did not and this seemed to satisfy her.

We both stood there silent and perplexed.

MY HAIR

I

"I think I'm gonna grow my hair long," I remember telling my mother.

"O no you're not," she said.

But O yes I was, and did.

I did what I wanted. I did what I felt was natural and right. I shook off the rest as a dog shakes off water.

Even as a metalhead, I was always a punk.

II

My mother worked as a secretary in the building we lived in.

I would visit the office to pick up my lunch, which was often a tuna fish sandwich wrapped in a paper towel with a can of Yoo-hoo on the side—still, to my mind, the perfect lunch.

Once, a tenant sitting at her desk turned as I entered and stared at my hair, and fell silent.

Big bulk. Frantic frizz. Dubious do swallowing my skull.

"This is my son," my mother said.

For further explanation, she offered, "He's a rocker."

III

I never really liked my long hair. I rarely, if ever, thought I looked good in it. It's possible I looked good and didn't realize it.

Once, walking the halls in high school, I heard a girl behind me say, "I wish I had hair like that." It was thick, preposterously thick.

Ironic.

I am now bald as a honeydew.

IV

When I got into hardcore, loyal to my belief that integrity is everything in this world, I did not cut my hair. I had no desire to cut my hair. In 1986 at CBGB's, I was one of the few longhairs. We stood out.

Skinhead, skinhead, skinhead; longhair.

I looked like a metalhead, but was always a punk.

WHAT IS THIS

On the floor of my mother's bedroom, directly under the window, sat an old and cruddy suitcase turntable that played not only 33 and 45, but also 78 RPM. I enjoyed sitting before it and listening to her Barry Manilow records, to the songs he wrote that made the whole world sing. I, too, sang.

One day I carried into her room the first album by Black Sabbath, borrowed from my sister's shelf. I placed it on the platter and touched the needle down. Waiting for the music to begin, I became aware that it had started to rain. Through the rain bells were ringing, which seemed odd. I knew that if the window were open I would see only the building opposite mine, six stories of red brick. I looked down at the turntable and music thundered into the room.

I know it now to be a G chord, followed by a flatted fifth, otherwise known as "the devil's interval," or "the devil in music," a minor progression banned during The Middle Ages as it was considered ugly and unpleasant and did not praise God. Its power was unquestionable.

In this room my father had slept with his sickness the first five years of my life, had left drops of blood on the sheets we could not afford to discard, on the towels bearing the hospital's logo we could not afford to discard.

The dark spirits in the room gripped and held me. Listening to this record for the first time, this dark sound released the year I was born, I was captivated. I was claimed. I was born.

SLAVE TO THE POWER

Gary, an older metalhead in the neighborhood, had bumped into my mother in the lobby. She told him where I was and he came and found me.

"Are you fucking psyched?" he screamed down at me in my seat.

I was every bit my mother's child, quiet and calm, and incapable of returning this kind of enthusiasm; I think I nodded.

Iron Maiden was my favorite band in the world. I worshipped them, and here I was sitting in the orchestra at Radio City Music Hall, the concert about to begin, my first concert ever. I was fourteen. It was January of 1985.

When Iron Maiden took the stage the entire audience sprang up and grew taller all at once, folding down their seats and standing on top of them. My mother did the same, and chanted along with Bruce Dickinson, and clapped her hands, and didn't get down from her seat until the show was over. She was a real Trooper (pun intended).

Winter was brutal that year. The roads were iced over and my mother was not thrilled with the idea of driving into Manhattan, but she did it to make me happy, to help me realize a passion. She seemed able to sense a genuine one, though she had little time in her life to discover any of her own.

My father's death a decade earlier had sent our lives spinning; it instilled in me a strong belief, an irrevocable one: I believed in Nothingness. It was all I saw.

I was the world's humbled guest.

Nothing belonged to me; Nothing was out there waiting. But I took joy in music: it won me over; it lifted me up.

I couldn't put it into words then, but I resolved that, in the face of Nothingness, the only hope was to create art, to create something that could *last.*

III

SIGHTSEEING

Hardcore is, at its best, phenomenal music in an intimate setting. Intimacy is crucial.

For example, I remember seeing Adrenalin O.D. at CBGB's in 1986.

Some skinhead mouthed off to the bass player and the bass player reached down from the stage and punched the skinhead in the face. Little surprises like that were the perks of seeing hardcore shows.

FINALLY

In 1986 Agnostic Front packed CBGB's like no other band. At the back of the dance floor and off to the side there was a couch I would stand on to watch the show.

I would be dripping with sweat the entire time just standing in that one spot, watching. As the show was winding down I was already anticipating the slow walk past the bar, down the narrow aisle stuck with bodies, until finally I could step outside, through the mine-like dark, into the bright light of day, where the cool air would wipe my face.

OUTERWEAR

In 1986, watching Agnostic Front play at CBGB's, I was intrigued by Roger Miret's tattoos. He had the name of his band carved into his chest. Below it Jesus hung on the cross, a gas mask on his face. A mushroom cloud rose in the background. Spiderwebs grew out of the singer's elbows.

    I was intrigued by his street look, his street existence. I never thought I would inhabit a world where tattoos are as common as white underwear.

    Today, even pop stars look like punk rockers, but punk rockers that have undergone a full spa treatment.

    Spiderwebs grow out of their gleaming elbows.

SUNDAY IS GLOOMY

At 3pm the doors would open and the crowd would funnel through. It was a slow but dignified process—dignified in the sense that no order was imposed upon the manner of entry. Once inside you paid your five dollars at the desk.

To approach CBGB's was to step inside a gathering of punks and skinheads out front, maybe some longhairs (I was one of them), and maybe even some people who weren't easily described in one word, all standing around on the street talking to friends, waiting to get in. It was extremely social. You would move around mingling, talking to this person or that one.

It was this way when I started seeing bands there in 1986.

The police line began in 1988. I remember seeing it for the first time as I approached on Third Avenue. There was no familiar cluster of people standing outside to enter into, to disappear into, leaving the rest of the city behind. There was a single-file line stretching away from the club and around the block, and that line of pathetic souls was standing behind a barricade.

That line, I knew, was the beginning of the end.

The lack of community outside extended into a greater lack of community inside, where more and more new recruits, blind to art, misinterpreted the ferocity of the music as a call to violence.

The doors closed for good on hardcore matinees the following year.

SIGN OF THE TIMES

Speed was my thing. Fast music.

When a band is fast and tight, the running together of speed and precision is as impressive as anything else music can offer up.

What's puzzling is that modern hardcore borrows very little not only from punk, but from traditional hardcore, whose essence was speed. It's not punk rock played at increased tempo, but metal played with decreased proficiency and gobs of bravado.

17 APRIL 1988, CBGB'S

That was the day one of "the twins," as they were known in the hardcore scene, punched me in the face. My knees buckled, but I righted myself quickly.

The twins were a set of identical bodybuilding skinheads who came into the scene and terrorized it, swinging chains and hammers on the dance floor.

Actually, my knees only buckled the third time I was punched.

After the first punch I glanced past my attacker at what looked like a stadium full of skinheads behind him, as many bald heads as there are waves in the ocean, it seemed.

After the second punch I asked myself if throwing a punch back might be the right thing to do here, at that same moment realizing I'd never thrown a punch at someone because I *had* to.

And at the third punch my knees buckled, but I righted myself quickly.

Then, as my nose had started to stream blood, I was whisked off, by several people at once as I remember, through the dance floor and past the side of the stage, downstairs to the bathroom so I could clean myself up. A guy hanging out down there suggested I shouldn't blow my nose, as it looked broken.

The Gorilla Biscuits 7" came out that day. I know I still had it when I arrived home that evening. It's possible it was with me the whole time. I can easily imagine myself washing the blood off my face with the record tucked gently under my arm. I was serious about supporting the bands I liked. Those records were important to me.

I was brought out through the back of the club. Apparently, there was a mob out front waiting to kill me. The police were called in. But nothing else happened.

Soon I was standing in front of the club side by side with my attacker. He mistook me for someone else, he explained. I told him it wasn't a problem.

He was lying though. This had been building.

I was accused of asking a girl he knew if he thought he was a real skinhead, implying, of course, that he was not, that he was, in fact, a "bonehead," a skinhead only in mimicry. A guy wearing the uniform. There were so many of those.

I'd never said a word, but he wanted a piece of me.

As we stood there in front of CBGB's one of the cops approached him and stared him down. "You again?" the cop scowled.

My attacker moved away slowly. As he did he looked back at the cop long and hard, with disgust and hatred. It was a look I've never given anyone in my life.

I GOT A RIGHT

The year was 2006. Liz and I decided to stop into CBGB's for a drink. I wanted her to see the place; she'd heard me talk about it so often. It was like showing her the house I grew up in.

We had to go now. We had to go while we still could.

Inside, I saw that Brendan from SFA was sitting at the desk. Though I knew it was him, I asked, "You're Brendan, right?"

"Yea," he said, and made a play of putting up his fists.

"My name is Lew," I said, and put out my hand. "Our bands played together a long time ago at the Lismar Lounge. I was in a band called Our Gang."

"O yea," he said, "that's going way back."

I introduced Liz and explained that she was from Texas and had never been inside the club before, that I wanted to show her around. I was only making conversation; I didn't expect to be invited in for free; I was more than willing to pay the door.

But he told us we were welcome to go through.

We took a seat at the back, across from the bar, in the elevated section where bands sold merchandise. I watched Liz. I watched her eyes scan the walls, reading graffiti, reading stickers. I took her picture.

We seemed to have a camera with us everywhere we went in those early days of our relationship. Soon it was pointing at me. I obliged, though I didn't like being photographed there. There was, of course, the implication that this photo must be taken now, to document a past life, in a place that would soon be of the past. But it also made me feel like a tourist.

This was a home to me. A place of belonging. Of deep roots. And I was grateful that Liz got to see this.

That, upon returning home, I had been invited in, as was my natural right.

IN ONE CITY

On Thursday nights Crucial Chaos aired on New York University Radio. I would sit in the living room of my apartment—the signal was strongest there—and listen on my boombox, recording live performances and interviews with local hardcore bands:

Altercation ... Gorilla Biscuits ... Krakdown ... Life's Blood ... NY Hoods ... Rest In Pieces ... Side By Side ... Straight Ahead ... Token Entry ... Underdog ... Warzone ... Youth Of Today ...

Then the antennae on my radio snapped off. Each week, I would touch it to the base when the show began, drawing in the sound. I held it in place for the duration and continued to record all the New York bands I was seeing live on Sunday matinees at CBGB's.

I didn't have any conscious desire to preserve these recordings for history. I wanted to preserve them for myself. I wanted to be able to listen again.

There were times when my friends were hanging out but I stayed home to record. There were times when out of town bands came through and I stayed home to record.

Fifteen years later, when I found the tapes in a box, I bought a tape deck and hooked it up to my computer and began to digitize, saving the files as MP3s and sharing them on the internet.

People flipped out over the stuff. People still flip out over this music that was created a quarter century ago, in one city, with listeners spread throughout the country and the world that, added up, *might* equal in number the population of one small American town.

That's my cassette you listened to, with the fragment of *Reign In Blood* poking through where I paused for a commercial then recorded again.

I went to lengths to sustain this music that was mine in my youth, to breathe new life into this music that is mine still, and I take great pride in this, as the artists went to lengths to bring it into being.

AN UNDERSTANDING

I was fifteen the first time I went to CBGB's. Straight Ahead was my first show. I had picked up a flyer at a record store in the city and brought it to my mother. It advertised a "hardcore matinee." She took this to mean it had something to do with pornography. The other band names on the flyer—*Crucifucks* and *White Plastic*—did not ease the odd impressions she was forming in her brain.

"It's music," I explained.

She let me go.

You had to be sixteen to get in. After walking through the front doors I was stopped at the desk by a woman in a housedress. I had a five dollar bill in my hand.

"You look very young," she said. "Are you sixteen?"

I assured her that I was, but she wasn't buying it. She decided to call my house to find out the truth.

My mother lied for me. I got in.

In between bands, a homeless man approached me outside the club. He looked like he had been rolling around in the street.

"What are you doing here?" he asked. "I know you're not from around here. I can tell just by looking at your skin that you're young."

I pointed to the club. "I'm here for the music."

This seemed to satisfy him. He shook my hand.

IV

AT THE MOVIES

I

In hardcore music, the band and the audience are one: they share attitudes; they share the stage; they share respect. Hardcore music rejects the idea that the band is superior.
    From the beginning, Bad Brains were a different story. CBGB's, 1982.
    H.R. walks out from behind the stage and steps off into the crowd with the swagger of a living legend; he knows it and they know it.
    "Monstrously tight and musical and exhilarating and inspirational" is how Jerry Williams, producer of the legendary ROIR cassette, described the band in *American Hardcore*. Ian Mackaye from Minor Threat described their live show as having "transcended anything" he'd ever seen; John Joseph from the Cro-Mags described it as a "spiritual experience," and MCA from the Beastie Boys described it as "magical."
    Bad Brains penetrated and thrilled the perceptions of their listeners in a way that was uncommon, seemingly more than human; it spoke of another world, of endless possibility; it represented mastery.

II

It's past four in the morning when I put on the DVD; H.R. walks out from behind the stage with the swagger of a living legend; when the crowd sees him they start to shout; "The Big Takeover" begins; the band explodes into music and the audience explodes into movement; H.R. is craziest of all; his dancing is savage; it is the perfect illustration of the music; he flails his arms and kicks his legs and when he sings he pounds his fist on his thigh in perfect time with the downbeat of the snare; he acts out the music; it becomes louder to the ear, more intense.

The audience is beside themselves; they are in a state of rapture; they, in their individual awkwardness, attempt with their bodies to illustrate the music; their movements celebrate the self; they dance like asylum inmates; they improvise a response.

Music can be understood in the reaction it inspires in bodies. Much of today's hardcore music is acted out as formulaic aggression. Bad Brains were acted out as pure exhilaration.

VICTIM IN PAIN

I

The first time I saw the cover to Agnostic Front's *Victim In Pain*, which features a Nazi soldier about to shoot a Jew in the back of the head, the Jew sitting on the lip of a mass grave, I wasn't sure what to make of it. I wasn't sure what to make of it at all. The year was 1984. I was fourteen.

It was the most *real* thing I had ever seen on the cover of a record. These were the days when the word "punk" still followed the word "hardcore." In true punk fashion, the cover was intended to shock, and it did. I wasn't sure what to make of it and put it back down in the stacks at my local record store, but the startling image lingered in my brain.

II

"There's no justice / It's just us / Blind justice / Screwed all of us" and "Remember we're a minority / And every one of us counts." The graphic image on the cover of Agnostic Front's *Victim In Pain*, illustrating the worst men can do to each other, have done in history, does not line up with the lyrical content, which calls for unity among members of the hardcore scene, who are outcasts from society. It could be that the man with the gun to his head represents a member of the hardcore scene, and the soldier represents the society that doesn't understand him and wants to destroy him.

III

An explosion rocks the Lower East Side of New York City. Manhole covers blow clear. Rats scatter through the streets.

The bursting intro chord that begins the title track to Agnostic Front's *Victim In Pain* never fails to jolt the system; the thick-fuzzed bass line that races out underneath it never becomes less frantic. *Victim In Pain* never stops being the greatest New York Hardcore record of all time.

It's raw and dirty, as New York City was then, not slick and polished, as New York City is now, as hardcore records are now.

It's genius songwriting, though the playing is ordinary; it's clear that what made it onto vinyl is the entirety of the band's capabilities; it's clear they possessed exactly what was needed and no more, which is to say that on this record they achieved the maximum outcome possible with what little they had; they took what little they had and shaped it into greatness.

DAVE INSURGENT

I

Around 1990 a punk band from Australia called The Hard-Ons was staying at my friend Billy's apartment. They were on tour in support of their album *Love Is A Battlefield Of Wounded Hearts*, the follow-up to *Dickcheese*.

The New York shows ended their tour. They were in no rush to leave. They lived in Billy's apartment for two months.

I was in a band called Gutwrench then. Billy was the singer. It was a great time, hanging out with those guys every day, doing whatever, playing whiffleball, going to shows, records stores, sitting around the apartment.

I remember once we were in the East Village talking about how great a band Reagan Youth was and at that very moment we spotted Dave Insurgent, the singer, walking down the street. We had been talking about wanting Reagan Youth shirts. We ran up to him—there were at least six of us—and asked him how we could get some. He'd been walking at a quick pace, as if towards something urgent, and jumped back at our approach. He was sorry but he didn't have any Reagan Youth shirts, he said, and was off again in a rush, God knows to what.

His heroin addiction is well-documented, as is his relationship with a prostitute who supported their life and drug habits by turning tricks while Dave, born David Rubinstein, waited on the street. And if you were to read up on him you would discover that he not only used drugs but sold them as well, often consuming most of what he was meant to sell, then defying the dealers he owed money, resulting in his being severely beaten with a baseball bat. He was hospitalized in a coma and received a frontal lobotomy to save his life.

In June of 1993 his girlfriend was picked up by a client and did not return. Dave searched for her in all the city's hospitals. The police did nothing to help. Her body was found days later decomposing in the truck of Long Island serial killer Joel Rifkin.

Two days later Dave's mother was accidentally run over by his father as he backed out of their driveway in Queens. She died in the hospital.

A few days after that, Dave Insurgent took his own life.

II

One of Reagan Youth's songs, "Anytown," opens with Dave Insurgent speaking over the guitar intro, asking his mother, "Where's Spot?" Spot is the family dog. He then realizes and exclaims with surprise, "He ran away!" And in an unexpected turn, as the song kicks in he encourages the dog to run further, snarling with attitude, "Run Spot run! Run Spot run!"

The lyrics go on to describe the milkman arriving at 6am, the singer waking up with a frown. "Another day in anytown." The verse is delivered lazily, communicating the boredom of repetition. It's not until the refrain, "Run Spot run!" that the voice lifts in excitement.

The second verse continues to illustrate the singer's contempt for common American life: "I called up Sally, Dick, and Mark / We took my dog Spot to the park / We watched him run and heard him bark." And once again the dog is encouraged to escape: "Run Spot run!"

In the third verse the singer confesses to his father feelings of sadness. The father suggests that the son is going mad, and the refrain of the song is now directed at the singer rather than the dog, as his father instructs, "Take him away! Take him away!"

III

Dave Insurgent died at the age of twenty-eight. A heroin addict. I wonder if the difficulty of achieving an independent, idealized life apart from society fueled his addiction. Or was it simpler? The drugs took over, leaving no room for the person, the man who carried the idea. Or was his life, and death, the realization of the idea in all its ugliness?

Reagan Youth's guitarist, Paul Cripple, born Paul Bakija, attests that the drugs took away "all his creativity, all his humor, all his goodness."

On top of addiction there was cruel fate, delivering two crushing blows, seeming to urge the singer to leave the earth.

Though he had recovered from his hospital stay at his parents' home in Queens, as soon as he was able he returned to life on the Lower East Side.

The song ends with the return of that initial guitar riff, the band slowing down behind it, as Dave Insurgent declares, "I don't want to live in anytown." And when the band comes to a full stop, he calls out with authority, "Anytown just makes me frown!"

V

OUT THERE

It wasn't simply that we didn't know how to tune our guitars; we weren't even in the neighborhood of being in tune; we were miles away, on the outskirts of the city; there was no road, only darkness, and the anguished sounds of frightened animals.

Some nights, Hobi would sit jamming with headphones on, bobbing his head as though he was playing his favorite song, but I could hear that what was going into his ears sounded like the scraping together of rusted machinery. Eventually the guitar would be passed to me and I, too, with hope, would play. The sound was excruciating, but I *was* holding a guitar; there was the implication of greatness, of what *could* be done if only the instrument might begin to cooperate.

Not knowing how to tune, we wrote whole songs. We invented our own chords and learned to move them around the neck. Already we were getting a whiff of immortality.

FULL FORCE

I had written some music for an OUR GANG song that came to be called "Energy."

Our singer, Bryant, wrote lyrics and arranged them to the music, then called me on the phone to share what he had come up with.

I'll never forget that.

He put the phone down next to his stereo, played a tape of the music, and ran around his room screaming the words.

The song was fast, the vocals fierce, but during the chorus he lifted himself above the melee and stretched a beautiful melody across the top before diving back down into the mayhem.

It's a mesmerizing experience, hearing the thing you've created elevated by the skill of another, feeling the thing you've created is the best thing ever in the world.

DEMO DEMO

The first time we visited Don Fury to record OUR GANG live to two-track, Hobi and I struggled to tune the bass and guitar to each other for our first take. We hadn't been playing long.

Don Fury scolded us. We didn't take the scolding lightly; this was the guy who had recorded *United Blood* and *Victim In Pain*.

On that first version of our *Uprising* demo, the out of tune bass and guitar reverberate with a horrible wobble, sounding like a distortion-smothered sneeze.

Of course we released the tape anyway.

It was a thrill to have a demo for sale at Some Records. I would sit around the store waiting for someone to buy a copy. When it finally happened I wasn't there, but I do apologize to whoever it was that had the misfortune of being our first, of popping that curdled cherry of a cassette.

By the time we returned for our second session six months later, with the addition of Javier on bass, Hobi and I now fulfilling our destiny as the double-axe attack, we had improved remarkably; it's amazing to look back on the stride we had taken in that short time. We re-released the demo from that session and this version sold well and is the recording we are known by.

The appeal of a demo tape is that it represents a band at a particular moment in time, usually at the most unselfconscious moment in their history. The band is hungry to be recorded and heard; it's what they want the most.

That was the case for me and Hobi with OUR GANG. The dream of our band defined us. It was the most important thing in our lives.

OUR GANG LIVE ON WNYU

From what I can gather, Johnny Stiff, the guy who booked bands for WNYU's Crucial Chaos, was not well-liked. The Dayglo Abortions, in their song "Kill Johnny Stiff," wrote that they wanted to "cut his balls off and feed them to pitbulls ... as payment to the bands." They didn't like his green pants and paisley shirt, and referred to him as a rip-off shithead promoter.

I wouldn't know about any of that. I never got as far as being in a touring band. But I remember Johnny Stiff calling my apartment and inviting OUR GANG to play live on WNYU.

My mother answered the phone and told me I had a call. I took it in the kitchen.

It was a shock. We were kids head over heels in love with the music we were making, but we didn't have a dream in the world of it being recognized. He liked our tape, he said, and asked if we wanted to play live on the air.

The night we played Crucial Chaos was my first night of college. I had just turned eighteen. I was taking night classes my first semester, not because I was working during the day, but because I was a bum and wanted to remain so. I slept during the day. Other than being in a hardcore band, not much was going on in my life. I didn't want anything else to be going on.

My buddy John Lisa picked me up at school and drove me to the city. Sitting in the back seat of his car was a non-threatening Peavey amp. I would be playing that on the radio.

We were cutting it close. The band was waiting on me. To my surprise, so were a few dozen of our friends from the hardcore scene. We barely had room to stand in the studio with our instruments. Though our playing was horrible, our sound awful, our friends, the crew in the studio, sang along with intense passion, screamed and applauded in between songs.

Fifteen years later, revisiting the cassette of this atrocity, I was finally able, for the first time, to get past what we lacked as a band, and remember, and properly experience, the fun we had that day.

LOOKING OUT

In May of 1989 OUR GANG opened for Token Entry at The Pyramid Club on Avenue A. We were, needless to say, the first band on the bill; I don't think we ever played a show where we weren't the first band on the bill. But we were, in fact, on the bill, and this gave me the right to loiter inside the doorway of the club in between bands. It was something I always wanted to do.

All the scene celebrities did it.

I remember consciously deciding to stand there, leaning my shoulder against the door frame, looking out at "the kids" on the street, looking across at Tompkins Square Park.

GOING OFF

Walking to The Pyramid Club, I bumped into Jules, the singer for Side By Side. The conversation came around to the fact that Side By Side needed a bass player. I offered my services.

"Do you go off when you play?" he immediately asked.

Did I jump around a lot when I played? That's what he was asking.

Did I jump high in the air when I played, pounding the air with my fist?

Did I make psychotic faces when I played, demonized by the music's fury?

Did I scream the lyrics when I played, scream them straight down the crowd's throat?

"Yea, I go off," I said. "You know, if I feel it, if the music moves me."

One look at me and I'm sure he could tell I did not go off.

I was shy and pudgy, fearful of dramatic movements, which tended to make my flab jiggle.

We went our separate ways at The Pyramid Club and never spoke again.

SITTING AROUND THE FIRE

The year was 2010. I walked into my sister's house to the horror of a large chunk of my family sitting together listening to OUR GANG's *Uprising* LP, a collection of live demo recordings made over twenty years ago.

The mellow crackling of the needle in the grooves in between songs, amplified by the silence in the room, was possibly more unbearable than the songs themselves, which were one and two minute bursts of poorly recorded, lightning fast noise.

I explained to my Uncle Bob, when he asked how many records we had sold, that only five hundred were pressed, that this music was meant for a select audience.

He asked if by select I meant the deaf.

17 JULY 2010

I

Liz described the atmosphere in the room as "magnetic." When we took the stage I felt the buzz. The floor was packed with old friends. I walked back and forth shaking hands.

After playing together for the last time in 1989, OUR GANG reunited in 2010 for a show at The Mercury Lounge celebrating the release of *Everybody's Scene*, Chris Daily's book about The Anthrax Club in Connecticut.

A late addition to the show, we were squeezed in as the third band and allowed twenty minutes. These twenty minutes we rehearsed, on and off, for four months. When the time came to show what we had prepared, we nailed it. The people felt it and let us know.

It wasn't yet midnight before I was back in the apartment with Liz, having a drink. "It's gonna take a few days to come down from this one," I remember her saying.

II

I'm standing still.
 I'm digging in.
 I'm picking fast, precise, even strokes; the sound jumps off the speaker and sticks in the air.
 It's like the air around me swells.
 It's like the air around me explodes. I'm making it explode.
 I'm digging in. You've got to. You've got to strike the string exactly right, or you're nothing.

The string answers back.
 The speaker answers.
 The empty space in the room answers.

It's like there's wind at my back.
 It's like I'm running with the bulls.
 It's like I'm tumbling in a dream.
 My body swells. My body is about to explode.

VI

A BRIEF, QUIET MOMENT

The year was 2011. I was on my way to Building 3S at The College of Staten Island to teach a class in Basic Writing when I ran into Mark Geissler. I recognized him right away, though we'd never met. He was a Facebook friend. Or maybe we did meet, once, through a mutual friend in the music scene, twenty years ago.

"Professor Dimmick!" he said.

"Mark! What's up?"

We shook hands.

Wardance Records had released a four-song EP from my new band, My Rifle. He told me he bought the record and thought it was great.

I thanked him. "That's really nice to hear," I said. In fact, it was the last thing I expected to hear. My mind was on introductions and conclusions, run-on sentences. We talked for a few minutes and went our separate ways.

I walked to Building 3S. In the few minutes it took me to get there, before entering the classroom and greeting my students, before going through the motions of earning my living, I allowed myself a brief, quiet moment of pride.

WHERE I WAS

I sat down with my bass. I had been working on my book and I was wondering if I would complete it or if anyone would ever read it and I started jamming on the strings and feeling some grooves and bending the strings and noodling around and sliding up and down the neck switching back and forth between my fingers and a pick finding melodies and getting tangled up in them then spinning loose and this went on for several minutes without pause and when I finally came to and realized where I was it was only then that I knew how long I'd been gone and it came immediately back to me that I was wondering if I would complete my book or if anyone would ever read it.

THE SOUL IS THE FORCE

The soul is the force that runs behind the chords. The notes are few to choose, but the soul is unending, the soul makes rhythm, the soul sings.

The soul is the force that runs behind the chords, and the notes, and the picking fingers, and the fretting hand, that owns the space after one note ends, before another begins, that owns the air between the hands and the wood as the hands close in, are made to move.

THIS MUSIC

This music that amplified my life.
This music — this art that
survives death, opposes death, that is
the furious opposite of death.

This music. These roots. This tribe.

I walk through my silent house,
this music in my body.